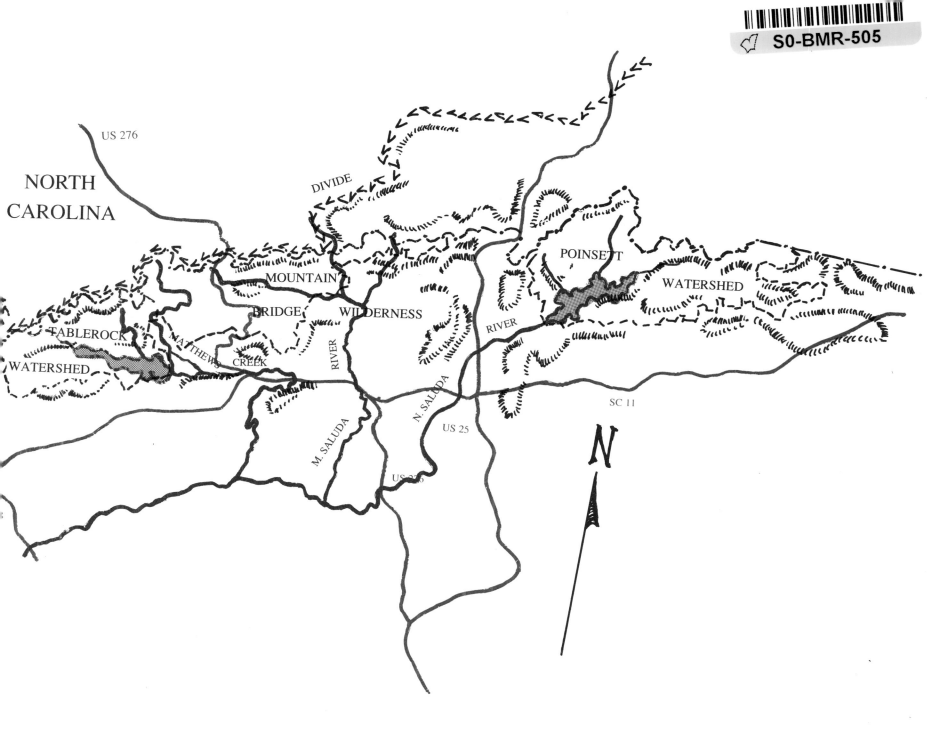

SOUTH CAROLINA'S
MOUNTAIN WILDERNESS

THE BLUE RIDGE ESCARPMENT

T. Blagden

SOUTH CAROLINA'S MOUNTAIN WILDERNESS

T. Wyche

THE BLUE RIDGE ESCARPMENT

Photography by Tom Blagden, Jr. and Thomas Wyche
Text by Thomas Wyche

Sponsored by The Daniel Foundation and Milliken & Company
in cooperation with The Nature Conservancy of South Carolina

WESTCLIFFE PUBLISHERS, INC., ENGLEWOOD, COLORADO

ACKNOWLEDGMENTS

Buck Mickel and Roger Milliken are two leaders in South Carolina whom I most admire and respect for reasons too numerous to outline here. It is an honor The Daniel Foundation and Milliken & Company chose to sponsor this book.

Two of the trustees of The Daniel Foundation, Buck's wife, Minor, and their daughter, Minor Shaw, are also very special friends and I am grateful to them for their support. I hope and believe that they, as well as Roger, will be pleased with what their sponsorship has produced.

The Nature Conservancy, of course, needs no introduction. Its South Carolina Chapter has been a major force in permanently preserving mountain regions and other vital natural areas around the state. My thanks to Patrick Morgan, executive director of the state chapter,

Rainbow Falls (T. Wyche)

for his critical involvement with the conservation easement protecting two Greenville watershed tracts — the "crown jewels" of the Mountain Bridge Wilderness. My thanks also to Pat's predecessors and to the staff in the national office who worked with Naturaland Trust during the early years of the Mountain Bridge project.

Full credit and deep appreciation must be given to the property owners whose cooperation made the Mountain Bridge Wilderness possible; to the Greenville Water Commission and the Greenville City Council, whose wisdom and foresight led to a conservation easement for the Greenville watersheds; and to the Duke Power Company, which has wisely managed its lands and opened them to the public for recreational use.

It has been great working with and learning from Tom Blagden, a true professional photographer and artist. In the process of photographing the Mountain Bridge and adjacent areas, I hope he may have discovered a new natural wonderland in his home state.

— T.W.

This book is very much the product of a collaborative effort and partnership. I especially want to thank Tommy Wyche for inviting me to participate in a project which he conceived and developed.

I have been fortunate to have worked previously with Westcliffe Publishers and The Nature Conservancy of South Carolina, both of whom bring the highest standards to environmental publishing. At Westcliffe my appreciation goes to John Fielder, Suzanne Venino, and Leslie Gerarden. At The Nature Conservancy, Pat Morgan, executive director of the South Carolina Chapter, has been an indefatigable ally to the project and helped shape its evolution.

Many other people assisted me in ways too numerous to properly acknowledge here. Please know that they are an integral part of this book, and to them I am most grateful: Heyward Douglass, Steve Hill, Nicole Jones, John Garton, Judy Cromwell, Dottie Schipper, Luke Platt, Jon Holloway, and Ben Keys. The following organizations and agencies also offered invaluable support: the Duke Power Company, Greenville Water Commission, South Carolina State Parks, and National Forest Service.

— T.B.

International Standard Book Number: 1-56579-056-1
Library of Congress Catalogue Number: 94-60962
Photographs © Tom Blagden, Jr. All rights reserved.
Photographs © Thomas Wyche. All rights reserved.
Text © Thomas Wyche. All rights reserved.

Published by Westcliffe Publishers
2650 South Zuni Street
Englewood, Colorado 80110

Publisher: John Fielder
Editor: Suzanne Venino
Designer: Leslie Gerarden
Proofreader: Bonnie Beach
Printed in Singapore by Tien Wah Press (Pte.), Ltd.

First Frontispiece: Falls along the upper Middle Saluda River, Jones Gap State Park, Mountain Bridge Wilderness (T. Wyche)

Second Frontispiece: Autumn colors near Lake Jocassee, Duke Power Company lands (T. Blagden)

Third Frontispiece: New York fern and rhododendron, Camp Greenville, above Jones Gap State Park (T. Blagden)

Title Page: Redbud trees, Sumter National Forest (T. Wyche)

T. Wyche

HEADFOREMOST FALLS, TRIBUTARY OF MIDDLE SALUDA RIVER, JONES GAP STATE PARK

7

MOUNTAIN LAUREL, CAESARS HEAD STATE PARK, MOUNTAIN BRIDGE WILDERNESS

T. Blagden

CONTENTS

SUNRISE FROM BAD CREEK, DUKE POWER COMPANY LANDS

T. Wyche

RILEYMOORE FALLS, CHAUGA RIVER SCENIC AREA, SUMTER NATIONAL FOREST

FOREWORD

Education takes many forms. It can come in a well-run classroom with a creative teacher and innovative lessons. And it can come from reading a book, researching a paper, doing homework with a parent, or attending a seminar. But learning, properly conceived, should be a lifelong and life-fulfilling experience not confined to books and schoolwork. Education can and should occur through every interaction we have with the world around us. An understanding of our world requires — perhaps more than anything else — knowing the natural world that is the ever-present backdrop for our activity.

This book is about one exceptional piece of that natural world: the Blue Ridge Escarpment of South Carolina. It is virtually impossible to capture the grandeur of this place in just words. Happily, the glorious photographs and accompanying text of this book are able to do justice to its majesty.

One reason the escarpment's natural features are so impressive is that they are unspoiled by the heavy hand of human development. Sitting in the middle of the fastest-growing region of the country (within minutes of the Greenville-Spartanburg area, less than two hours from Charlotte, and three hours from Atlanta) are 40,000 acres of undeveloped and preserved mountain land — the Mountain Bridge Wilderness and two vast adjoining watersheds.

Nearby, the Chattooga enjoys protected status as a National Wild and Scenic River. Other neighboring lands and watercourses, such as the Chauga River, are deserving candidates for similar designation. This book, in one sense, is about these unprotected places as much as it is about the protected ones, for it offers a lesson, a subtle but powerful instructive message that these areas also must be preserved.

But why should we work hard to make available the opportunity to camp, hike, bird watch, fish, and simply relax in the fresh air and open spaces? There are many obvious answers to this question. The trees we preserve create the air we breathe. The species of plants and animals we save may yield tomorrow's medical cures or help maintain the ecological balance. But additionally, as this book portrays, there is value in beauty itself, and natural sites like the Blue Ridge Escarpment are places of beauty that we need to maintain for future generations.

Of particular interest to me is the educational potential of these pure and untarnished lands. In our schools today, there is a proper emphasis on "environmental education," but only so much of this type of education can be acquired in the classroom. Just as no father can teach his child about fly-fishing unless there are free-flowing streams that hold trout, neither can one who studies plants, birds, or other animals get more than a basic introduction to a subject through lectures, texts, and films.

We learn about living *with* nature only by being *in* nature. We learn of its power by viewing a waterfall or riding whitewater rapids. We learn of its beauty while sitting in a wildflower meadow. We learn of our role on this earth by climbing a mountain, exploring a cave, or camping under a night sky filled with a million stars.

If you could ask Henry David Thoreau, or any hiker who has navigated by compass, he would tell you that natural places teach self-reliance. Jack London, or anyone who has encountered surprise conditions in the wilderness, would tell you that natural places teach tenacity and cleverness. Thomas Jefferson, or any American who has treasured the land as a source of nurturing and spiritual regeneration, would say that natural places teach the values of respect and responsibility.

The teaching force of nature inspired the poetry of William Wordsworth and the wise counsel of Rachel Carson. The natural world inspired and permeated the writings of Hemingway and Emerson. It was in nature that Francis of Assisi saw the hand of God. All of these people, and innumerable others, found learning — indeed, transformation through edification — in natural places.

This book tells the tale of one majestic natural place that will stand preserved for all time — a testimonial to the work and commitment of Tommy Wyche. While serving as Governor of South Carolina in the 1980s, I was pleased to play a supportive role, together with President Jimmy Carter and Secretary of the Interior Cecil Andrus, in helping to ensure the preservation of these lands.

In this stunning collection of words and pictures, Tommy Wyche and Tom Blagden treat us to a sampling of nature's finest. Having themselves been educated by and about this remarkable area, they in turn are teaching us about South Carolina's beautiful Blue Ridge Escarpment and the need to preserve more places like it.

— Richard W. Riley

A native of South Carolina, Richard W. Riley has long been concerned with environmental and educational issues. As two-term governor of South Carolina, he spearheaded a comprehensive and highly successful reform of the state's school systems. In 1992 Riley was appointed U.S. Secretary of Education by President Clinton.

T. Blagden

JUMPING OFF ROCK ABOVE LAKE JOCASSEE, A RESERVOIR OWNED BY THE DUKE POWER COMPANY

PREFACE

I was most fortunate as a young man to have grown up in rural South Carolina and to have spent most of my summers and many wonderful winter weekends on the valley floor beneath Caesars Head. Our family's cabin was located near the South Saluda River in the community of Lakemont. Those endless summer days, which don't seem so long ago, allowed me to gain a true appreciation for South Carolina's mountains and their wonders.

We "gigged" for frogs in the cool mountain night air, fearing possible attacks by gigantic poisonous snakes. Many times I hiked to the top of Table Rock, expressing excitement to my companions about the possibility of seeing black bears or perhaps a mountain lion. Then there was the unforgettable first youthful encounter with a massive timber rattlesnake.

I remember the Saturday nights we square danced to our favorite bluegrass tunes. On Sunday mornings outdoor inter-denominational services were held at Lakemont, where families singing traditional hymns accompanied by a whining antique bellows organ reminded me of what it must have been like a century ago.

Images of water rushing over smooth river rocks bring back memories of water so cold you dare not enter except on the hottest of summer days. I trekked with friends over spectacular mountain passes where fall colors were so breathtaking that they still remain indescribable. And the quiet times, spent reflecting on the events of each day and making plans for the future, were invaluable to me. My memories are frozen in this time and place. They can never be taken from me, they will never be forgotten.

I was indeed fortunate to have spent my formative years in these mountains, and now, through The Nature Conservancy, I am actively participating in the protection of South Carolina's majestic mountains, including areas along the Blue Ridge Escarpment.

Thankfully, my childhood memories will never fade. I have the luxury of being able to revisit such special places as Caesars Head, Lakemont, and Table Rock Reservoir, among many others. These places and adjacent areas have remained essentially the same, intact and functional, because of the efforts of one man — Thomas Wyche.

In 1972, Greenville attorney and community leader Thomas Wyche (Tommy to his friends and associates) developed the concept of creating the Mountain Bridge Wilderness. To do so, he established Naturaland Trust, the first land trust in South Carolina. Tommy also drafted the South Carolina Heritage Trust Act, the first legislative trust in the United States, and he played an important role in protecting the Chattooga as a National Wild and Scenic River. With the help of his son Brad, Tommy authored a booklet delineating methods of preserving lands within the state. In addition, he was selected as South Carolina's Environmentalist of the Year in 1979 and received one of ten Gulf Oil National Conservation Awards in 1983.

Tommy, whose personal commitment to conservation is unparalleled within South Carolina, truly exemplifies the Conservancy's credo of "quietly protecting nature." The preservation of such a magnificently diverse area of the Blue Ridge Escarpment is a tribute to his foresight, dedication, and perseverance. In essence, this book represents the culmination of his accomplishments as a conservationist, nature photographer, and author.

After publishing *South Carolina's Wetland Wilderness: The ACE Basin*, the Nature Conservancy of South Carolina is proud to be a participant in a second book with Westcliffe Publishers and Tom Blagden. The Conservancy is grateful to the two co-sponsors, The Daniel Foundation and Milliken & Company, for providing the cornerstone for this project.

"When I learned that the South Carolina Chapter was involved in yet another wonderful book, I was overjoyed," commented Joe Williams, Chairman of The Nature Conservancy's Board of Governors and a native of Camden, South Carolina. "The quality of photographs and the text allows the reader to understand further the need to nurture and conserve these glorious mountains.

"The Nature Conservancy was active in protecting a large portion of this region, consisting of special areas like this one. We are one of many 'partners in conservation' who have helped protect invaluable mountain acreage and produce this tribute to the natural beauty and uniqueness of the Blue Ridge Escarpment in South Carolina."

This region is a part of The Nature Conservancy's long-range, five-state Southern Appalachian conservation initiative. This endeavor is one of the largest, most complex conservation initiatives ever conceived in North America and is similar in scope and design to the Conservancy's efforts in the Yellowstone Park region and the Ouachita Mountains in Oklahoma and Arkansas.

The South Carolina mountains and their pockets of wilderness provide a natural sanctuary unmatched in its grandeur. To hike, camp, or live in these sacred mountains is an experience that will remain with one for a lifetime and, hopefully, for future generations.

— Patrick H. Morgan

Patrick H. Morgan is Executive Director of The Nature Conservancy of South Carolina. A certified wildlife biologist, he has directed the Conservancy's state program for the past four years. Morgan, a native of South Carolina, is an avid photographer and bird watcher with an affinity for all of the natural treasures of his home state.

T. Wyche

A SPECIAL PLACE

Let's take a stroll, or even a strenuous hike, into an extraordinary piece of our planet Earth — the Blue Ridge Escarpment of South Carolina. This is wild and rugged country. A place of craggy peaks, precipitous walls, and forested ravines. Raging whitewater rivers course over house-size boulders and mountain streams cascade down rock-strewn slopes. Waterfalls abound. Within this tortuous terrain are gentle areas as well, small springs and quiet glens, flowered trails and silent pools.

Tucked into the very northwestern corner of the state, along the rocky borders of North Carolina and Georgia, the Blue Ridge Escarpment of South Carolina encompasses some 150,000 acres, a wonderland of natural features created eons ago as tectonic plates collided and caused the land to buckle. Over the centuries, rain and water, in enormous amounts and with inexorable force, sculpted the heart-stopping showcase of scenery visible today.

Water plays a dominant role, with rainfall in these mountains exceeding that of any other region of the country except the Pacific Northwest. Here, however, most days are sunny; rainy weather seldom lasts long, although storms can bring torrential downpours. All of this moisture pays enormous dividends. Teeming life is everywhere — pulsating, thriving, and growing. There are more than 1,600 species of plants, 67 bird species, 60 species of reptiles and amphibians, and 429 aquatic insects — two of which were recently discovered and are believed to be new to science. Black bears, making a remarkable recovery from near extinction, roam the forest. Deer, foxes, beavers, and raccoons are found here as well. In remote places inaccessible to the logger's saw stand giant trees more than two centuries old.

This is a special place, a place that I first discovered many years ago camping in the mountains with my family — hiking on shaded woodland trails, swimming in icy rivers, and singing around the campfire. For countless summer weekends our favorite adventure was paddling canoes down frothing whitewater rivers, especially the Keowee, Toxaway, and Horsepasture before they were dammed to meet our endless energy needs. The Chattooga River was the most exciting ride, but the rugged beauty of the Chauga holds enduring memories.

Now a third generation of my family sets up their tents, finds firewood, listens to the tree frogs in the rain, and sings along with a harmonica after roasting marshmallows. They hike beside sheer rock faces and along mountain ridges high above rivers, slowly gaining an appreciation of nature.

Our language is woefully inadequate to articulate the subtle changes that these outdoor experiences bring about in a person — the gradual awareness and deep appreciation of the natural world, the recognition of being a part of something much larger than oneself. I have a firm conviction that the individual, especially a young person, who spends time in nature will develop quite a different perspective of the world, along with a sense of balance and inner serenity. As one of my daughters claims, "It makes you a three-dimensional person."

I have had the good fortune to take backpacking and river trips in other states and countries. Visiting these wild places only strengthened my realization that the Blue Ridge Escarpment is indeed extraordinarily special. Yet because of its ruggedness and inaccessibility, many of its natural wonders are known to only a few. Wanting to share the beauty of the area, I started thinking about the idea of a book.

At the same time, I was aware that these mountains would not always remain as they are today. I became intrigued by the idea of permanently preserving this special place to ensure that it would remain unspoiled for others to enjoy as my family has throughout the years.

In 1973 I established the Naturaland Trust as a legal entity for the effort to preserve 40,000 acres along the escarpment. Its motto became its mandate: "a few special places...in trust for the future." With support from the private sector, the cooperation of various state agencies, and The Nature Conservancy, the pieces of the puzzle slowly came together over a twenty-year period to create the Mountain Bridge Wilderness.

As envisioned from the start, the Mountain Bridge Wilderness would form a "bridge" between, and include, two vast watersheds owned by the City of Greenville. This final piece fell into place in 1993 when the city and the Greenville Water Commission, in partnership with The Nature Conservancy, protected these watersheds with a permanent conservation easement. The watersheds, along with the lands acquired through the efforts of Naturaland Trust, now preserve almost one-third of the escarpment in South Carolina.

Enlisting support for this project meant giving talks and slide shows to local civic groups, conservation organizations, and garden clubs. The research and visual materials gathered for the presentations grew into a book. And here it is!

The Blue Ridge Escarpment of South Carolina is a special place that becomes more special by the way we perceive it. Perhaps this book will enhance our perception of these mountains and of others as well. So join us on a journey into South Carolina's mountain wilderness.

SUNSET, TABLE ROCK AND THE RESERVOIR BELOW, SEEN FROM CAESARS HEAD

MORNING FOG ON TOP OF COLDBRANCH MOUNTAIN IN THE MOUNTAIN BRIDGE WILDERNESS

WILDNESS AND WILDERNESS

Vertical walls and deep ravines ... the Escarpment

The Blue Ridge Escarpment, a treasure of mountain and river landscapes, reaches from Georgia to southern Virginia. Throughout its 70-mile stretch across South Carolina, the escarpment towers at elevations of more than 3,000 feet, reaching its zenith at 3,554-foot Sassafras Mountain, the state's highest peak.

While other mountain ranges reach greater heights, most of them come to earth more gradually. In contrast, the Blue Ridge Escarpment ends abruptly, plummeting in dramatic 2,000-foot cliffs to the foothill region known as the Piedmont.

Just what is an escarpment? The technical definition reads: "a steep cliff formed by erosion or by a fault." Perhaps a more apt description comes from the Cherokee Indians who lived in the shadow of the mountains; they called this place "Blue Wall."

Within its brief span through South Carolina, the escarpment boasts four state parks, a federal and a state wilderness area, two wild and scenic rivers, a national forest, and two federally designated scenic areas, as well as both private and public lands protected as preserves or through conservation easements. Remarkably, the entire escarpment within South Carolina, some 150,000 acres, is managed by only four entities: the U.S. Forest Service, the State of South Carolina, the City of Greenville, and the Duke Power Company.

Wild rivers and foaming shoals ... the Chattooga and Chauga

Hidden within the escarpment are many diamonds in the rough: pure rivers — multi-faceted, of high purity and white color — formed in deep ravines. Here, where the rivers make abrupt, sharp turns, foaming waters churn over rock ledges and crash into vertical walls before racing over granite shoals and settling into deep pools. For a moment, they become emeralds or sapphires before resuming the frenetic, headlong flight to less tumultuous places.

The only way to see these sparkling jewels is to clamber down the steep sides of a gorge, clinging to saplings or bracing against tree trunks. These off-trail hikes, usually only 400 to 500 feet in length, are arduous and require sturdy boots, strong legs, fierce determination, and — especially — a sense of adventure.

In 1974 Congress designated the Chattooga a National Wild and Scenic River. The Chattooga's turbulent waters and renowned whitewater rapids draw rafters and paddlers from around the country. Notwithstanding its wild nature, the river offers relatively easy access and is one of the main attractions of the area.

Fed by rains that exceed 90 inches per year, the Chattooga gains momentum in North Carolina for 10 miles and is a full-fledged river by the time it becomes, at Ellicott's Rock, the boundary of South Carolina and Georgia. Above the S.C. Highway 28 bridge, no paddling or floating is permitted; this section of the river is reserved for anglers and hikers. The Bartram, Foothills, and Chattooga trails afford ample opportunities for exploration.

Below the bridge, the Chattooga is placid for seven miles until it reaches a shallow crossing known as Earle's Ford. This is the starting point for Section 3, as boaters have dubbed the 17-mile stretch to the U.S. Highway 76 bridge. Here the Chattooga picks up pace, and both the beauty and the danger increase every few miles as the river swirls through rapids such as Rock Gardens, the Narrows, Eye of the Needle, Roller Coaster, and the thunderous Bull Sluice, a perilous rapid which marks the end of this section.

Mounds of fresh snow floating on Matthews Creek,
Mountain Bridge Wilderness (T. Wyche)

But more awaits you ... much more. Section 4, the seven-mile stretch to Lake Tugaloo, is one of the country's most challenging whitewater runs, particularly for open boats. Rapids here bear the names Screaming Left, Seven-Foot Falls, Corkscrew, Jawbone, and Sockemdog, all rated in the most difficult class of rapids. Below Sockemdog lies Dead Man's Pool, a macabre name which is sadly appropriate, for every year or so a paddler drowns trying to navigate Sockemdog. For those who wish to experience these sections of the Chattooga in a less dangerous fashion, numerous outfitters offer trips in larger, more stable rafts — a safe yet exhilarating way of seeing and sensing the pulse of a great whitewater river.

Dogwood blossoms, Table Rock State Park (T. Blagden)

Not as long or as large as the Chattooga but equally as pristine and rugged, the Chauga River flows just a few miles to the east. The Chauga runs free for only 20 miles before being swallowed up by Lake Hartwell, but during that short distance it drops 800 vertical feet, crashing over a chaotically fractured riverbed that twists through sheer granite gorges. Downstream from Blackwell Bridge there is usually enough flow for a whitewater adventure comparable to the Chattooga. In fact, because of the constricted passages, tight turns, and steep drops, many experts consider the Chauga as difficult to navigate as the lower sections of the Chattooga.

The U.S. Forest Service has designated a narrow corridor on either side of the Chauga as a scenic area. This designation can be revoked at any time, however, and efforts to have the Chauga permanently protected as a wild and scenic river have been unsuccessful. Intense logging outside of the area has already increased the turbidity of the water and deposited debris along the riverbanks, scars which threaten the beauty of the river. Hidden within deep ravines, the Chauga has not received the widespread public recognition it deserves, yet this untamed river — with all its twists and turns and narrow gorges — epitomizes the unspoiled wildness of the escarpment.

Precipitous walls and roaring cataracts ... a land of waterfalls

The combination of a vertical landscape and prodigious amounts of rain creates a mesmerizing effect. Nearly everywhere you look along the escarpment are scores of waterfalls dropping from sheer cliffs, cascading over boulder-strewn slopes, and splashing down mountainsides. Some are well-known, others are nameless — yet all cast a magical spell.

Probably the most impressive waterfall on the escarpment is Lower Whitewater Falls, a roaring wall of water that plummets 400 feet and carries the highest volume of water of any waterfall in the area. It is just a short distance from the shore of Lake Jocassee and can be seen from a platform that affords a dramatic head-on view.

A ten-minute walk from U.S. Highway 276 takes you to the lovely Brasstown Falls, a series of four cascades that stair-step some 70 feet. Near the Chattooga River, within a 30-minute walk of Burrell's Ford Road, Kings Creek Falls also plunges 70 feet. Requiring a little more exertion, Licklog Falls (also known as Pig Pen Falls) and Long Creek Falls can be seen from the banks of the Chattooga. Isaqueena Falls, with its 100-foot drop, is only a short distance off S.C. Highway 28 near the forest ranger station.

Fed by Tamassee Creek, 90-foot Lee Falls claims the title as Oconee County's prettiest waterfall. It can be difficult to find and requires a steep climb up a rugged and unmarked trail, but the effort is well worth it, for after a rain the waterfall splits into three plumes. The Forest Service has designated Lee Falls as a federal scenic area.

Bottle gentian growing near the Table Rock Reservoir (T. Blagden)

Nearby, an easy 20-minute walk from the road, Station Cove Falls cascades 60 feet, and in springtime myriad wildflowers color its banks. Like all of the waterfalls along the escarpment, Station Cove Falls possesses its own special charm.

Protected and partly tamed... hiking trails and man-made lakes

Hiking trails wind throughout the mountains of South Carolina, following river drainages, climbing high ridges, and meandering through sun-dappled forests. The Bartram Trail, named after the noted botanist William Bartram, traces the Chattooga River through Sumter National Forest. It then crosses into Georgia and North Carolina.

Beech leaves in Matthews Creek (T. Blagden)

The other major route through Sumter National Forest is the 90-mile Foothills Trail. From Oconee State Park it travels north along the Chattooga River and passes through the Ellicott Rock Wilderness, a 9,012-acre wilderness area that straddles the boundaries of South Carolina, North Carolina, and Georgia.

Ellicott Rock is named after noted surveyor Andrew Ellicott. On assignment for the State of Georgia, he set out in 1811 to locate the 35th Parallel, thereby establishing the boundary between Georgia and North Carolina. A large rock on the east side of the Chattooga River bears the markings "LAT 35 a d 1813 NC = SC." This is commonly perceived to be Ellicott's Rock, but this perception may be at odds with reality; the date on the rock is two years after Ellicott finished his work, which was related to the Georgia-North Carolina boundary not to the South Carolina-North Carolina border. In his report, Ellicott paid grudging tribute to the terrain his survey team encountered: "...the difficulties and hardships partly owing to the mountainous face of the country have exceeded anything I have ever before experienced."

Ellicott Rock Wilderness and the surrounding mountain lands suffered from heavy logging many years ago and, as a result, no significant virgin forests remain. In the many years since the last logging operations, however, the area has gradually been restoring itself, and in a few more decades these forests will regain their earlier grandeur.

Filigree of decaying leaves (T. Wyche)

Construction of nearly half of the Foothills Trail was funded by the Duke Power Company, a major landowner in the region. The company owns large holdings in the area around and including Lake Keowee and also about 50,000 acres within the escarpment. This property adjoins the eastern edge of Sumter National Forest from the South Carolina-North Carolina boundary to the Lake Jocassee Dam.

Lake Jocassee is a 7,500-acre reservoir of cold, emerald-green water enclosed by the steep walls of the escarpment. The once free-flowing waters of Horsepasture and Toxaway Rivers now lie buried beneath the lake, with only vestiges of these rivers still flowing downstream from North Carolina. Most of the Thompson River has also been confined by the dam, although a mile or so runs wild in South Carolina, twisting through a deep canyon that challenges the most adventuresome explorers. Boats on Lake Jocassee can nose their way into the spectacular gorges carved by these tributaries.

Accessible to the public by Devils Fork State Park, Lake Jocassee is a wonderland of outdoor recreation: swimming, water skiing, sailing, and scuba diving are just some of the water sports available here. Anglers work Jocassee's waters for trout and smallmouth bass. Boating across the lake will take you to the Laurel Fork and Thompson River waterfalls.

(Continued on page 22)

The lands along the escarpment owned by the Duke Power Company serve primarily as watersheds for Lake Jocassee and for the smaller 360-acre Bad Creek Reservoir, pumped-storage reservoirs used to generate electricity. Water from Lake Jocassee flows through huge tunnels, dropping some 310 feet under tremendous pressure to turbines and generators at Lake Keowee, an 18,500-acre reservoir downstream. At night, when energy demand diminishes, water is pumped back up through these tunnels to Lake Jocassee, ready to be released the next morning to generate power for the awakening public. In conjunction with a nuclear power plant located on Lake Keowee, Duke Power has assembled a facility capable of generating more than 4.3 million kilowatts of electricity, making it one of the largest energy producers in the world.

The "Cathedral" festooned with icicles, Mountain Bridge Wilderness (T. Wyche)

In 1980 Duke Power donated a 373-acre tract of land along the Eastatoee River, another tributary of Lake Jocassee, to the Heritage Trust for permanent protection. This gorge and its surrounding lands are the centerpiece of one of South Carolina's first Heritage Trust Preserves, a state program to protect outstanding natural areas. It is home to a forest of old-growth hemlocks, several rare plants (including the tunbridge fern, which exists nowhere else), and a self-sustaining trout population. Nestled within the preserve on the banks of the river lies a beautiful campground. Hikers can scramble downstream a short way to see the river narrow to only a few feet, pressed in by vertical rock walls. Nearby, Reedy Cove Falls seems to split into two separate waterfalls, hence its other name — Twin Falls.

The Duke Power Company's management of its holdings on the escarpment has enhanced and protected the natural assets of the area. Nearly all of its property is logged for timber, and the company's planning included planting a second-growth forest to replace harvested trees. The power company has worked closely with the State Wildlife and Marine Resources Department and with groups representing hunters, anglers, hikers, and backpackers to allow full use of their property for outdoor recreation. Duke Power, in an example of corporate and community responsibility, has managed its lands to provide both power and pleasure for the public good.

Stewardship and vision . . . the Mountain Bridge Wilderness

Adjoining the Duke Power Company property on the east is the final segment of the escarpment in South Carolina, the Mountain Bridge Wilderness. This state-managed area encompasses some 10,000 acres, forming a "bridge" between two vast watersheds owned by the City of Greenville. Together these lands form a 40,000-acre wilderness preserve.

At the western end of the Mountain Bridge is Table Rock Reservoir, completed in the 1930s, and on the east is the Poinsett Reservoir, built in the 1950s. Recognizing the inextricable link between the quality of water and the quality of its source, the City of Greenville had the foresight to acquire not only the lake beds but also their surrounding watersheds, totaling 9,800 and 19,000 acres, respectively.

Whitetail deer crossing Lake Jocassee (T. Blagden)

Over the years the Greenville Water Commission has been passionate in its protection of these lands, strictly enforcing the bright green "No Trespassing" signs posted throughout. The purity of the water flowing from these reservoirs has earned the City of Greenville the self-proclaimed distinction of having the "world's best water."

The city's stewardship of these lands allowed an ecosystem of unparalleled richness and diversity to prosper. During the summer of

1992, the water commission sanctioned the first biological assessment of the Table Rock and Poinsett watersheds. Scientists were astonished by some of their discoveries: old-growth forests; newly found champion trees (the largest of a species within a particular region); trophy-size brook trout; and a stunning variety of birds, reptiles, amphibians, and insects — many of them rare or endangered and two of them new to science. Their findings described the Table Rock lands as "impressive natural treasures...the most significant wilderness area remaining in South Carolina."

In 1993 the water commission and the City of Greenville granted a permanent conservation easement to The Nature Conservancy, thereby protecting these watersheds in perpetuity. As one of the nation's most important conservation achievements, this action protected some 30,000 acres of land, the largest area in the eastern United States — and the fourth largest in the country — to be granted conservation easement. It also assured the final pieces needed to complete the Mountain Bridge Wilderness, an undertaking started twenty years earlier with the vision of preserving a significant portion of the Blue Ridge Escarpment.

Established in 1973, Naturaland Trust, South Carolina's first land conservation trust, was formed with the goal of securing the privately owned mountain lands between the Table Rock and Poinsett watersheds. Over a five-year period the trust initiated negotiations with each of the 18 landowners who held tracts within this area. In 1978, Naturaland Trust presented a formal proposal to the State Parks, Recreation, and Tourism Commission outlining the concept for permanently protecting the nearly 40,000 acres along the escarpment by acquiring 10,000 acres from private owners and by securing permanent protection for the Table Rock and Poinsett watersheds.

Fog-enshrouded mountains in early morning, from Caesars Head State Park (T. Blagden)

With the support of Governor James Edwards and his successor, Governor Richard W. Riley, the proposal was approved and acquisition of the various properties began. With just two exceptions, all of the landowners donated half of the value of their property to the state, thus enabling South Carolina to fund land purchases solely with Federal Land and Water Conservation Funds. Today, only a single tract of 1,200 acres is needed to fully complete the "bridge."

Lands acquired through Naturaland Trust form the very heart of the Mountain Bridge Wilderness, a paradise for nature lovers that counts three state parks within its boundaries: Caesars Head, Jones Gap, and Table Rock.

Table Rock State Park adjoins its namsake watershed. Its unique attraction is a 1,000-foot granite monolith which takes its name from the ancient beliefs of Native Americans that gods dined on the massive rock while sitting on the "Stool," a smaller mountain nearby. The park has a lake for swimming and boat-

Rappelling down the 300-foot face of El Lieutenant, Mountain Bridge Wilderness (T. Wyche)

ing, and a popular restaurant overlooking the lake serves old-fashioned "country style" fare. Well-marked trails suitable for children lead hikers along scenic streams. A more strenuous hike climbs to the top of Table Rock; from there visitors gaze straight down to the reservoir hundreds of feet below.

Jones Gap State Park lies on the banks of the Middle Saluda, South Carolina's first state designated wild and scenic river. Here, the state has refurbished an old fish hatchery where visitors can view 24-inch brown and rainbow trout lazing in the pure, cold water.

Perhaps the most popular spot in the Mountain Bridge Wilderness is the summit of Caesars Head, within Caesars Head State Park. From the viewing station atop this 3,266-foot peak, visitors can practically see forever, looking across the escarpment to the west or out onto the foothills to the east. Matthews Creek descends 1,200 vertical feet

Shelf mushrooms, also known as chicken-in-the-woods, growing in the Mountain Bridge Wilderness (T. Wyche)

through a deep gorge known as the "Dismal." The updrafts formed here make this a favorite fly-over for hawks and other raptors; in the fall of 1992 observers at the Caesars Head overlook counted more than 4,000 hawks. A portion of Matthews Creek has been protected by the Watson Heritage Trust. This 1,600-acre preserve contains the state's only mountain bog, with six rare plant species, including swamp pink, bog rose orchids, and the climbing fern.

Within the Mountain Bridge Wilderness, as throughout the escarpment, are breathtaking waterfalls: Raven Cliff Falls plunges 400 feet into Matthews Creek; Headforemost Falls drops more than 700 feet down a series of rocky shoals; and Rainbow Falls, a popular destination for youngsters from nearby YMCA Camp Greenville, paints a spectrum of colors formed by sprays of cascading water.

Nearly 50 miles of hiking trails wind throughout the Mountain Bridge, and almost every path claims some outstanding feature: an overlook, a hanging cliff, a sheer rock face, a lovely waterfall, or a mountain ridge with panoramic vistas. Primitive camping is permitted along these trails in designated places.

A State Wildlife Management Area, the wilderness is open, during season, for deer, black bear, grouse and squirrel hunting. Turkey, eliminated many decades ago, were recently reintroduced and are now thriving here.

Such is the wildness and wilderness within the Mountain Bridge Wilderness and all along the Blue Ridge Escarpment of South Carolina. These 150,000 acres offer outdoor experiences ranging from the quiet and reflective to the exciting and arduous, from hunting and fishing to whitewater thrills, from short afternoon hikes to extended backpacking journeys. Above all, the beauty and diversity of the escarpment remains accessible to anyone who seeks to find what nature offers.

Allegheny spurge, a rare flower, Orchard Cove along the Eastatoee River (T. Blagden)

T. Blagden

Upper section of Brasstown Falls, Sumter National Forest

25

T. Wyche

EARLY MORNING SUN HIGHLIGHTS FERNS ON THE FOREST FLOOR, SUMTER NATIONAL FOREST

T. Wyche

SUNSET OVER POINSETT RESERVOIR

T. Blagden

Rock ledges of Slicking Falls, looking toward Table Rock, Greenville Watershed

T. Wyche

Aerial view of whitewater rapids on the Chattooga River, Sumter National Forest

T. Wyche

TREES STAND STARK AGAINST THE SKY, JONES GAP STATE PARK

30

NEWLY LEAFED TREES OF SPRING, MOUNTAIN BRIDGE WILDERNESS

T. Wyche

WINTER ALONG THE CHATTOOGA RIVER, SUMTER NATIONAL FOREST

T. Blagden

LOWER WHITEWATER FALLS, FROM THE FOOTHILLS TRAIL VIEWPOINT, DUKE POWER COMPANY LANDS
PAGES 34-35: WINTER TREES SEEN THROUGH A VEIL OF ICICLES, CAESARS HEAD STATE PARK

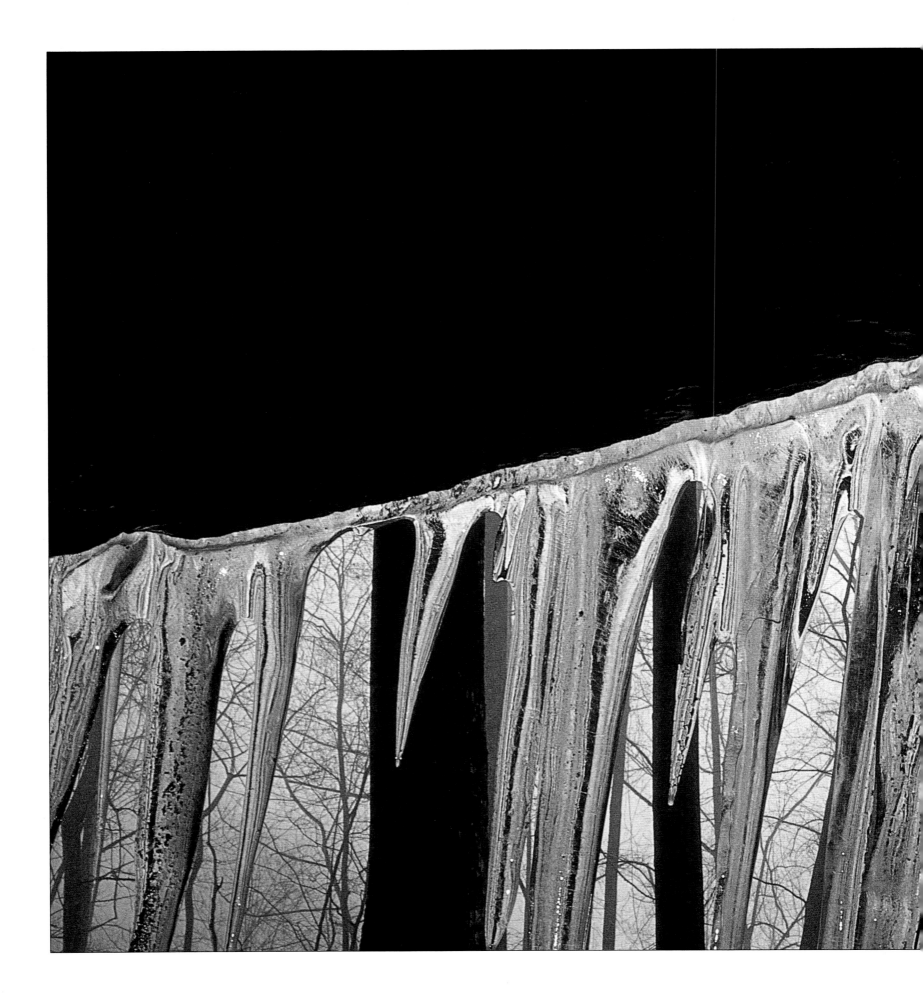

T. Blagden

T. Blagden

COMMON BLUE VIOLETS AND FALLEN REDBUD FLOWERS, STATION COVE, SUMTER NATIONAL FOREST

T. Blagden

TABLE ROCK RESERVOIR, GREENVILLE WATERSHED

FALLS CREEK FALLS, JONES GAP STATE PARK

MOSS-COVERED LOG ALONG THE CHATTOOGA RIVER

T. Blagden

ROILING RAPIDS AT BASE OF LOWER WHITEWATER FALLS, BAD CREEK, DUKE POWER COMPANY LANDS

T. Blagden

BLUETS AND CRESTED IRIS LEAVES, ALONG THE CHATTOOGA RIVER

41

T. Wyche

SPRING DOGWOODS, SUMTER NATIONAL FOREST

42

T. Blagden

LITTLE SWEET BETSY, STATION COVE, SUMTER NATIONAL FOREST

THE 30-FOOT-WIDE EASTATOEE RIVER NARROWS TO A FOUR-FOOT SWATH OF FOAMING WATER, PICKENS COUNTY

T. Blagden

LONG CREEK FALLS, AT CONFLUENCE OF THE CHATTOOGA RIVER

T. Blagden

OCONEE BELL, A RARE SPECIES, DEVILS FORK STATE PARK

T. Blagden

Pine needles and autumn leaves, the Chauga River, Sumter National Forest

47

T. Wyche

FEATHERY WHITE BLOSSOMS AGAINST FEATHERY WHITE CLOUDS, MOUNTAIN BRIDGE WILDERNESS

T. Blagden

WHITE RHODODENDRON, CAESARS HEAD STATE PARK

49

T. Blagden

TRANQUIL POOL AT THE BASE OF TABLE ROCK

50

THE FORCES OF NATURE

Although you need not be a scientist or geologist to appreciate the raw beauty of the Blue Ridge Escarpment, knowing a little about the powerful natural forces that created it may add an element of wonder to the experience of being enveloped in these mountains.

For its entire length, the Blue Ridge Escarpment is the easternmost edge of the Southern Appalachians. Here the mountains come to an abrupt halt, falling more than two thousand feet to the Piedmont below. How did this striking terrain come about?

Table Rock as seen from the reservoir below, Greenville Watershed
(T. Blagden)

The geologic history of the Appalachian Mountains stretches back in time more than a billion years. Long before the culminating episode that led to the formation of the mountains seen today, ancient mountain ranges once rose here. Over vast expanses of time, the mountains eroded, depositing layers of sediment into the ocean. These layers, buried and compressed over time, eventually became sedimentary rock. Enormous heat and pressure over millions of years then changed it into a harder, erosion-resistant "metasedimentary" rock.

Scientists theorize that the earth's crust is a rigid shell that is separated into about ten sections known as tectonic plates. All the world's land masses and ocean floors rest on these plates, which shift and move over time, creating changes in the earth's topography as well as changes in the position of continents.

The mountains we see today began forming about 300 million years ago when the North African plate collided with the North American plate, causing the land to buckle and push upwards. The inexorable forces of the tectonic plates crushing into each other formed the Appalachian chain along what is now the eastern United States. The extreme pressures and temperatures generated by this upheaval, which took place over 50 million years, were greatest in the areas closest to the line of collision. In some places, basement rock — the oldest, "original" rock in the area — was lifted over younger sedimentary rock. Eventually the North African plate slowly drifted apart from North America to become separated by the Atlantic Ocean.

Geologists are still studying and debating exactly how the Blue Ridge Escarpment was formed. With such cataclysmic forces of heat and pressure over such an enormous period of time, these mountains were not created in a uniform manner. A portion of the escarpment lies within a major fault zone of the Brevard Fault, and there are numerous minor faults as well. Over time these faults have caused the landscape to fall, tilt, and shift.

The escarpment's varied geologic past can be seen in the chaotic formation of cliffs, jutting rock faces, precarious ledges, and colossal boulders. Occasionally, large veins of white quartz intrude into rock fissures at haphazard angles. Flecks of mica can be seen embedded in rock or lying loose on the ground, sparkling in the sun like so many diamonds. Long parallel layers of rock stacked atop each other are apparent in waterfalls and cliff faces. Sometimes horizontal, sometimes tilted, or even curved, these layers were once part of a seabed, evidenced by the uniform thickness of the strata. Surprisingly, there are no signs of fossils. It could be that the intensity of mountain building forces obliterated any fossil remains.

Over the millennia, the mountains of the Blue Ridge Escarpment have felt the dramatic effects of weathering and erosion. Run-off from torrential rains sluicing over steep terrain carved deeply into the landscape. The escarpment averages more than 90 inches of rain annually. This abundant moisture combined with a moderate climate produced rapid plant growth, resulting in accelerated biochemical weathering of the landscape. These conditions eroded all but the most resistant rock. Softer rocks have long since disappeared, leaving behind the severe cliffs that characterize the escarpment.

Many of the rivers that flow over the escarpment have their birth on the eastern continental divide. This is an imaginary line that follows an irregular course along the mountains. Waters to the east of the divide eventually flow into the Atlantic Ocean; waters to the west drain into the Gulf of Mexico. The size and force of rivers and streams flowing over the escarpment vary considerably, depending to a large extent on the distance between the divide and the escarpment. In general, as the distance between the divide and the escarpment diminishes, rivers and streams become smaller.

The geologic history of South Carolina's Blue Ridge Escarpment is evident everywhere you look — in the precipitous walls, sheer cliffs, deep ravines, and plunging waterfalls. This dramatic scenery is startling evidence of great forces of nature, forces that over eons pushed pieces of mountain skyward and over eons wore them down. The Blue Ridge Escarpment is a geological classroom, and the lessons to be learned reinforce the awesome power of nature.

T. Blagden

ROCK LEDGES AT SLICKING FALLS, WITH TABLE ROCK IN THE DISTANCE

RAPIDS AND ROCKS ALONG THE CHAUGA RIVER, SUMTER NATIONAL FOREST

T. Blagden

RED MAPLE TREE IN SEED, EARLY SPRING ALONG THE CHEROKEE FOOTHILLS PARKWAY

T. Wyche

SUNRISE FROM PRETTY PLACE CHAPEL, CAMP GREENVILLE

55

T. Blagden

MIDDLE SECTION OF BRASSTOWN FALLS, SUMTER NATIONAL FOREST

RED LEAVES OF A BLACK GUM TREE AGAINST A BRIGHT BLUE SKY, MOUNTAIN BRIDGE WILDERNESS

T. Wyche

T. Blagden

MOUNTAIN LAUREL AND MAPLE-LEAVED VIBURNUM, CAESARS HEAD STATE PARK
PAGES 60-61: WRIGHT FALLS ON LAKE JOCASSEE, BELOW MUSTERGROUND MOUNTAIN

T. Blagden

MARGINAL WOOD FERN, HEART-LEAF ASTER, AND YELLOWROOT ALONG THE CHATTOOGA RIVER

T. Wyche

REEDY COVE FALLS, ALSO KNOWN AS TWIN FALLS, PICKENS COUNTY

T. Wyche

SUNRISE ON TOP OF TABLE ROCK, WITH THE RESERVOIR BELOW, MOUNTAIN BRIDGE WILDERNESS

T. Blagden

Maple trees in morning fog, near Rocky Bottom

T. Blagden

MAYAPPLE AND TRILLIUM, STATION COVE, SUMTER NATIONAL FOREST

T. Wyche

REFLECTIONS ON A PLACID SECTION OF THE CHAUGA RIVER

T. Blagden

RAINBOW FALLS, CAMP GREENVILLE

T. Wyche

REFLECTING POND OF BLUE HOLE FALLS, SUMTER NATIONAL FOREST

T. Blagden

LAKE JOCASSEE AT SUNSET, FROM JUMPING OFF ROCK, DUKE POWER COMPANY LANDS

T. Wyche

AERIAL VIEW OF HORSEPASTURE RIVER AND THE FOOTHILLS TRAIL FOOTBRIDGE, ABOVE LAKE JOCASSEE

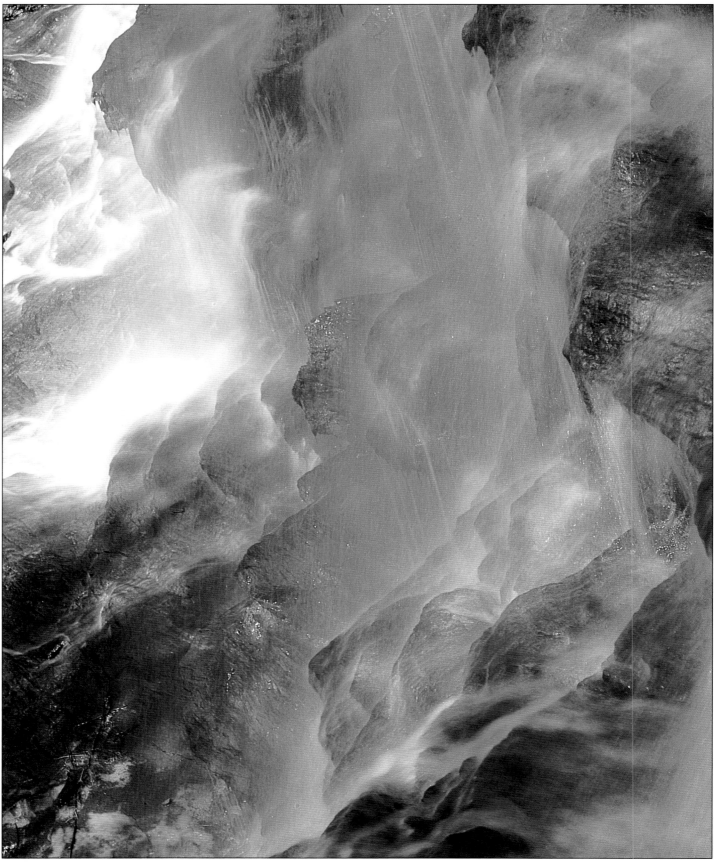

T. Blagden

ISSAQUEENA FALLS, SUMTER NATIONAL FOREST

T. Blagden

INDIAN PINK, TABLE ROCK STATE PARK

MAPLE TREES ALONG THE SHORE OF LAKE JOCASSEE, DUKE POWER COMPANY LANDS

INDIANS, EXPLORERS & PIONEERS

In the vast geologic time frame of the Blue Ridge Escarpment, humans have lived here for only the briefest moment. During that short period, however, extraordinary activity has taken place. There is evidence of human occupation of this region as early as 300 A.D., when it was home to an unknown group of Indians. Later came the Muskogeans and then the Etowahs. By 1500 the Cherokees had settled in the most habitable pockets of these mountains.

The Cherokees and neighboring tribes hunted the abundant wildlife, caught fish, and gathered fruits and nuts from the forests. Except for skirmishes between tribes, the Indians lived in harmony with each other and the land.

In 1540 a contingent of Spanish explorers led by Hernando de Soto disturbed the relative tranquility of the Blue Ridge. With an army of 570 soldiers, de Soto led vicious attacks on the Cherokees, torturing and killing, burning villages, taking women as prisoners, and forcing the chiefs to lead the expedition in its fruitless quest for the mythical El Dorado and its great stores of gold.

Although there is debate among historians as to the exact route that de Soto took in his long journey to the Mississippi, it is certain that he crossed the Blue Ridge Mountains. In a journal describing the expedition, special note was made of the terrain when his soldiers reached the escarpment:

> From Cutifachi to Xualla are 250
> leagues of mountainous country;
> thence to Guaxule, the way is over
> very rough and lofty ridges.

Studies suggest that Xualla was an Indian village in the vicinity of present-day Walhalla, the county seat of Oconee County, and that Guaxule was near the North Carolina-Tennessee border. Historians are divided as to where de Soto crossed the Chattooga River. Some claim that he climbed the Indian Winding Stairs Trail (now a hiking trail near S.C. Highway 107) and crossed the river at Burrell's Ford; others contend that his army crossed at Nicholson Ford (a few miles upstream from the S.C.Highway 28 bridge). In any event, de Soto did indeed cross the Chattooga and eventually found his way to the Mississippi in 1541. But the legendary El Dorado eluded him, and he died of fever the following year.

Today, it is difficult to imagine the mountain wilderness that the Indians and early explorers saw: mighty trees 30 feet around and towering more than one hundred feet; majestic herds of buffalo and elk; wolves, panthers, bears, foxes, and wild turkeys roaming throughout the forest; skies filled with countless birds and waterfowl; the brilliantly hued Carolina parakeet, now extinct, flitting among the trees. For the next several centuries, this was the scene that other explorers, hunters, traders, and settlers would find.

Green moss beside the falling waters of Reedy Cove Falls, Pickens County (T. Wyche)

By the mid-1700s, English fur traders from the coastal settlement of Charles Town arrived in the mountains, anxious to trade with the Cherokee, Creeks, and Catawbas. Fur trade with the Indians became the colony's most lucrative business, as skins and pelts traveled down the "Keowee Trail" to Charles Town. The fashionable in England, it seemed, could not get enough "South Carolina hats," made from upcountry deerskin.

A stable relationship between the British and the Cherokees was secured in a most improbable manner. An eccentric Scot named Alexander Cuming, who possessed no experience in Indian affairs, felt confident in his ability to quell tensions that had arisen with the Cherokees. Surprisingly, Cuming's mission was a success. Not only were the Cherokees impressed with him (his arrival during a violent thunderstorm didn't hurt), but they also agreed to send two chiefs and five warriors with Cuming to London. They arrived in 1730 to a great fanfare, and before leaving, the Cherokees signed a treaty with King George in which they promised to trade only with the English; in turn, the English agreed not to live or farm near Cherokee villages. Many peaceful and productive years of trade followed.

Two decades later the British aided the Cherokees in their fight against the French during the French and Indian War (1756 to 1763). The Revolutionary War (1776 to 1783) brought the Cherokees into even greater contact with outsiders. The British agitated the Indians to attack settlers in the area, and in 1777 the Cherokees mounted a major attack. With no established national or state government to call on for protection, the settlers organized their own fighting forces and defeated the Cherokees. This resulted in the Treaty of 1777 at DeWitt's Corner (now the town of Due West) in which the Cherokees ceded any claim to their remaining lands in the colony except for a narrow corridor along the Chattooga River.

Cinnamon ferns reflected in quiet pools, Greenville Watershed (T. Blagden)

For several decades Indians and settlers co-existed in relative peace. The influx of settlers continued, however, as more people moved into the area, taking over more and more land. A treaty with the federal government in Washington, D.C., followed by a treaty with South Carolina, led to the sale of the Cherokees' last remaining land in South Carolina in 1816. This tract consisted of 50,000 acres, including what is now a large piece of Sumter National Forest. The Indians were paid ten cents an acre.

During the next hundred years there were dramatic changes to the lands along the escarpment. Scottish, English, and German settlers migrated into the area from the coastal regions of South Carolina and from the valleys of Pennsylvania and Virginia. (Compare the English name "Westminster" with the German "Walhalla" — towns at the foot of the escarpment only eight miles apart.)

The first immigrants to the area settled in the flat valley bottoms and mountain coves. As more people arrived, and as families grew, it was necessary for them to move farther up the mountainsides. Tiny farms clinging to steep slopes were aptly described as "corn fields tilted to the sky." The virgin timber (with some trees more than six feet in diameter) was too large to cut and move, so the farmers worked "clearings" in the middle of the forests, small plots made by girdling trees — incising a deep cut all the way around the trunks, causing the trees to die. Eventually farmers took to burning trees to clear the land,

but without tree cover to hold the soil in place, farms were soon washed down the mountainsides. The family would then abandon the farm and start another, only to have the cycle repeated.

Life was hard. With little trade to support themselves, mountain people had to live off the land. The wildlife, hunted for food and clothing, diminished rapidly. The very mountains and cascading waters which had originally seemed so inviting now trapped people in a downward spiral of worsening conditions. Doctors and teachers were virtually unknown, and communication with the rest of the world, or even with neighbors only a few miles away over the next ridge, was difficult and infrequent.

The late 1800s brought hardship not only to the people of these mountains, but to the mountains themselves. Timber companies from the Northeast purchased large tracts of land in the Blue Ridge, and subsequent logging devastated the vast virgin forests. Debris left behind from logging operations became fuel for fire, feeding wildfires that inevitably swept through the forests. Without protective cover, the rich soils created over millions of years washed away, and erosion cut further into the landscape. Having exploited thousands of acres of forest, the timber companies moved westward. In the short span of only two generations, a natural Eden was laid waste in the Blue Ridge Mountains.

At the dawn of the twentieth century, many people living in these mountains found life to be bitter. Unable to produce an

Fallen hemlock at the base of King Creek Falls, Sumter National Forest (T. Blagden)

adequate income from farming their steep plots of land, mountain people turned to moonshining, the manufacture of illicit whiskey from homemade stills. (The word moonshine is derived from the practice of operating stills by moonlight so that the telltale smoke would not be visible to "revenooers," federal agents constantly on the prowl for such illegal operations.) Moonshining became a way of life for many, for a

Loss of trees and topsoil reduced the limited economic incentives that once lured settlers to the area, and the devastation of the land most likely prevented random development and subdivision. Perhaps it was for these reasons that large tracts of land could be assembled — and protected — during this century. Preserved as national forests, state parks, and wilderness areas, the lands along the escarpment are now returning to much of their former splendor.

The Chattooga River carves its way through rocky ledges (T. Wyche)

A still pool beside the rushing waters of the Chattooga River (T. Wyche)

crop of corn generated many more dollars in the form of "mountain dew" than as fodder for cattle or as produce to be laboriously hauled out of the mountains and taken to market.

By the early 1900s, many mountain people had abandoned their farms and moved on. Most of the wildlife was gone and the forests destroyed. It was time for nature to heal her wounds.

In response to the continuing destruction of vital natural resources, President Theodore Roosevelt, in a voluminous report to Congress in 1901, stressed the necessity of protecting the mountain regions of the South, including the Blue Ridge. He recommended the creation of a national forest system, and ten years later, the passage of the Weeks Act cleared the way for establishment of our first federal forests. Land acquisition on the Blue Ridge Escarpment began around 1912. Today, the Andrew Pickens District of Sumter National Forest manages 79,000 acres along the Chattooga River.

The harsh treatment inflicted on the Blue Ridge Escarpment during the last 150 years can, ironically, be viewed in a positive light.

T. Wyche

Host for parasitic mosses and mushrooms, a fallen log slowly decays

YELLOW BRANCH FALLS, OCONEE STATE PARK

T. Wyche

YELLOW LEAVES OF THE TULIP TREE CATCH THE LAST RAYS OF THE SETTING SUN, OCONEE COUNTY

T. Blagden

PINE TREE IN MORNING FOG, TABLE ROCK, GREENVILLE WATERSHED

82

T. Blagden

PEREGRINE FALCON SOARING ABOVE ITS NESTING SITE ON THE CLIFFS OF TABLE ROCK

LIGHT AND SHADOW, FALLS CREEK FALLS, A TRIBUTARY OF THE MIDDLE SALUDA RIVER

FRESH SNOW ALONG THE MIDDLE SALUDA RIVER, JONES GAP STATE PARK

DAY LILIES, POPULAR GARDEN FLOWERS, BRIGHTEN THE FOREST FLOOR, JONES GAP STATE PARK
PAGES 86-87: FALL FOREST IN A SOFT FOG, ABOVE ROCKY BOTTOM, PICKENS COUNTY

LAKE JOCASSEE AS SEEN FROM JUMPING OFF ROCK, DUKE POWER COMPANY LANDS

T. Blagden

THE CHATTOOGA RIVER, FROM RAVEN CLIFF, JUST BELOW LONG CREEK FALLS

T. Blagden

HEMLOCK TREES AND RHODODENDRON ALONG THE MIDDLE SALUDA RIVER, JONES GAP STATE PARK

T. Blagden

Morning fog, looking toward Table Rock from Caesars Head State Park

THE THOMPSON RIVER CATCHES ITS BREATH BEFORE PLUNGING DOWN A DEEP GORGE ON ITS WAY TO LAKE JOCASSEE

T. Wyche

LICKLOG FALLS, SUMTER NATIONAL FOREST

T. Blagden

LONG CREEK APPLE ORCHARD AFTER THE FIRST HEAVY FROST

T. Blagden

JUST A FEW APPLES REMAINING, LONG CREEK APPLE ORCHARD

T. Wyche

The Oconee Bell, endemic to the Blue Ridge Escarpment, Oconee County

T. Wyche

THE THOMPSON RIVER RACES THROUGH A GORGE TO LAKE JOCASSEE

T. Blagden

SUMAC AND TREES IN THE FOG, EASTATOEE VALLEY

HUCKLEBERRY AND AMERICAN CHESTNUT ON THE SUMMIT OF TABLE ROCK

T. Wyche

THE *YUCCA FILAMENTOSA*, NAMED FOR ITS THREADS, IS COMMON IN THE MOUNTAIN BRIDGE WILDERNESS

100

T. Wyche

BEECH LEAVES OF A SEASON PAST AND A BLOSSOMING REDBUD TREE, SUMTER NATIONAL FOREST
PAGES 102-103: CHRISTMAS FERNS AND TULIP POPLAR PETALS, EASTATOEE GORGE HERITAGE TRUST PRESERVE

T. Wyche

ICY WINTER SPRAY OF FALLS CREEK FALLS, JONES GAP STATE PARK

THE LURE

The Blue Ridge Escarpment lures beholders with its wildness, its beauty, and its diversity. It reigns in majestic ways — plummeting waterfalls, craggy peaks commanding panoramic vistas, cathedral spires of giant hemlocks. Beauty also lies in small vignettes — the shimmering silk of the spider's web, the eager bloom of the snow-dusted violet, the sunlight's dance on the fragrant foliage that mints the fresh mountain air.

If we allow, we can lose ourselves in this beauty. Sitting by a mountain brook, we see treetops mirrored in a quiet eddy. We note the brilliance, subtlety, and movement of color in the smooth water. We reflect on the stream's ceaseless flow and its prevalence and abundance in these woods.

The forest floor is a reservoir of water. Ample rainfall, captured by the sponge of the forest cover, slowly migrates into the soil and crevices in the rock bed. Years, perhaps decades later, these raindrops emerge as ooze that trickles into bogs, into springs, and on into streams drawn relentlessly toward the sea.

Scuffing fallen leaves during an autumn stroll in the forest sends them whirling before you, crisp and lively. As the seasons pass, the leaves become quiet and cling to the earth, but in their decay, they fuel the cycle of life.

The forest floor holds a buried treasure of centuries past, each layer covered by that of the following year — leaves, bark, twigs, and needles bequeathed by the press of nature's changes. Over time, tiny unseen filaments of ubiquitous fungus transform this detritus into nutrients to sustain the visible plant life above; it is the cornerstone of the life cycle of the forest. The invisible but pervasive fungi inexorably conquer all that once had life. Quietly absorbing organic matter, it speeds its return to the soil where it can give root to new life and produce the splendor we enjoy. From out of the earth and into the earth reaches the forest.

Above the ground, seeds of life are scattered in all directions, in countless numbers in countless ways. Maple and ash seeds glide through the air in aerial cavorts, dandelion and thistle seeds float on the wind in parachutes to earth, flowers emit fragrances that attract insects to carry their life-giving force away. Through the air, on the streams, seeds of plants are borne to be born. Miraculously and silently the creation of new life occurs.

We, too, can be re-created in these mountains. To perch on a cliff's edge far above the frantic world below, to come suddenly upon a deer and fawn grazing in a glade, to watch shafts of sunlight pierce the morning mist — each experience brings a primal peace. To see silver water splash down rocks and boulders, to discover the early spring blooms nestled along tree trunks, to muse with friends around a campfire — each experience renews the spirit.

An encounter with the wilderness is like other aesthetic experiences, be it art, poetry, drama, music, or dance. Perhaps in these mountains the experience is more intense because we are participants,

A monarch butterfly alights on an ironweed flower, Tamassee Creek, Sumter National Forest (T. Wyche)

not merely viewers or listeners. In these sylvan surroundings, we, too, appear on stage, giving an immediacy to the beauty around us.

Every experience in the forest builds upon previous ones and enhances the next. They all become permanent additions to our collection of memories. Each experience hones our appreciation of beauty, and this deepening sense of wonder enriches our lives.

There is pure form beauty in the wilderness. To ask "Why preserve wilderness?" is to ask "Why preserve beauty?" Thankfully, in this part of the Blue Ridge Escarpment, South Carolina's mountain wilderness and all its stunning variety is preserved and accessible to everyone. We can stand silent and still, hear the quiet, breathe the air, and sense the beauty that lies in all corners of these resplendent mountains.

T. Wyche

SHEER ROCK FACE BESIDE A NARROW HIKING TRAIL IN CAESARS HEAD STATE PARK

T. Blagden

LEE FALLS, SUMTER NATIONAL FOREST

T. Blagden

CATESBY TRILLIUM, JONES GAP STATE PARK

T. Wyche

Tamassee Creek, Sumter National Forest

T. Blagden

DWARF IRIS NEAR LAKE JOCASSEE, DUKE POWER COMPANY LANDS

T. Blagden

Raven Cliff Falls, Caesars Head State Park

T. Wyche

MATTHEWS CREEK CASCADING OVER BOULDERS, CAESARS HEAD STATE PARK

T. Wyche

LATE AFTERNOON LIGHT FILTERS THROUGH THE TREES, SUMTER NATIONAL FOREST

T. Wyche

PEELING BARK OF A RIVER BIRCH, PICKENS COUNTY

T. Wyche

STATION COVE FALLS, ONE OF THE MOST POPULAR WATERFALLS IN OCONEE COUNTY

T. Wyche

SOLITARY PINE CLINGS TO A 400-FOOT CLIFF, JONES GAP STATE PARK

117

T. Wyche

LEE FALLS, SUMTER NATIONAL FOREST

FERNS AGLOW IN A SETTING SUN, SUMTER NATIONAL FOREST

T. Blagden

SUNRISE FROM PRETTY PLACE CHAPEL, CAMP GREENVILLE

T. Wyche

FALLS CREEK FALLS, JONES GAP STATE PARK

T. Blagden

SLICKING FALLS AND RED-LEAFED SOURWOOD TREE, TABLE ROCK, GREENVILLE WATERSHED

T. Blagden

SUNRISE OVER THE FOOTHILLS, FROM THE SUMMIT OF TABLE ROCK

T. Blagden

BRIGHT GREEN MOSS BLANKETS A FALLEN LOG ON THE BANKS OF THE CHATTOOGA RIVER

T. Blagden

GREENBRIAR AND WHITE PINE, ALONG THE CHATTOOGA RIVER

T. Blagden

AUTUMN FOREST BELOW JUMPING OFF ROCK, DUKE POWER COMPANY LANDS

AFTERWORD

On the summit of Table Rock I gazed out over the reservoir 1,500 feet below. From my perch on the lip of the cliff, I surveyed the impressive expanse of wilderness to the north: Caesars Head, the Dismal, the Mountain Bridge Wilderness, and the primeval coves and slopes of the Greenville watershed. Suddenly, the shrill call of a peregrine falcon pierced the quiet. From far below, the bird floated skyward on updrafts along the cliff face, rising like a puff of smoke in the still air.

I could not have imagined the ensuing episode. For the next hour and a half, Heyward Douglass — a biologist, professional pilot, photographer, and frequent trail companion — and I sat mesmerized by the aerobatics of two adult and two young peregrine falcons. They soared laterally along the cliffs, climbed until they were just specks in the impeccably blue sky, and then plummeted in headlong dives and aerial chases truly fitting of the fastest birds on earth.

Heyward knew these birds. He had assisted other biologists in introducing peregrines to Table Rock to establish it as a peregrine nesting site, the only one in South Carolina. But Heyward had never seen anything like this. His appreciation intensified my own. The peregrines made us both feel lucky to be alive, sitting there on ancient granite before a pristine wilderness.

Elsewhere on Table Rock we explored rock balds and ledges. Ravens chortled and cawed, a sound synonymous with wild places and bold topography. At the top of the cliff we found an owl pellet of fur-encased chipmunk teeth. Numerous islands of moss had been charred black by lightening strikes, contrasting against the gray granite. Other moss beds were rolled back like a thick carpet by a bear's recent foraging. While I sat resting on a small patch of moss, Heyward peeled up the end of another and, to his delight, found a black widow spider. My inclination for a deep snooze on a soft mattress of moss immediately dissolved.

After a decade of photographing and living on the coast of South Carolina, I had difficulty comprehending that I was still in the same state. When I began work on this book, I knew almost nothing of the South Carolina Blue Ridge. Like many others, I had always jumped the border to North Carolina or Tennessee. I arrived at the "Blue Wall" innocent and ignorant, but with a fresh, hungry eye. I was immediately in awe of what I encountered.

I launched into this book project with much trepidation, for the subject was unknown to me. Yet once immersed in wilderness, I was consoled by an instant sense of familiarity. I had grown up in rural New England, where streams, lakes, and mountains comprised my world. Here, in the upcountry of South Carolina, I suddenly felt that I had come home again, and I was ready to embrace this mountain realm.

The bold, rugged geography of the mountains is vastly different from the soft edges and flat expanses of the coast: cascades and precipices contrast with the slow, rhythmic forces of tide and flatwater rivers; explosions of autumn color pulsating through the forest canopy contrast with the gradual, seasonal unfolding of hues along the shore; the mountain wildlife, elusive and often solitary, contrasts with raucous aggregations of waterbirds on the coast. Comparisons are inevitable because they are worlds apart, yet each embodies an integrity of place.

The dramatic topography itself commands my attention: cliffs, waterfalls, rapids, boulders, and forested slopes. Unlike the coast, the mountains exude a strong sense of form, and the irregular terrain requires varied perspectives. Perhaps most important, the mountains necessitate a physical involvement. Backpacking and arduous day hikes have a way of merging my senses and sensibilities with the environs. Sweat and perception often seem inseparable. To follow tumbling streams, drop from ridge to valley and then up again, is to know the land. I feel it in my muscles and bones, in every breath and smell. Even the pace is different from the coast; it becomes aggressive and charged, like the terrain itself. The photographic pursuit of waterfalls becomes an addiction, as their remoteness and power satiate a sensory hunger to experience the land.

South Carolina's Blue Ridge Escarpment holds three exceptionally beautiful lakes: Lake Jocassee, Table Rock Reservoir, and Poinsett Reservoir. All are man-made and are prominent features in the landscape. As a newcomer, the photographer in me sees them on a purely aesthetic basis — spectacular locations which defy their unnatural origin. Tommy Wyche, having spent a lifetime in these mountains, looks at these lakes and thinks of deep coves and whitewater rapids that he once knew firsthand that are now forty feet underwater. It is harder for him to maintain a photographic innocence.

Knowledge and perception are sometimes at odds with each other. Photographers must grapple with a paradox: our work deals with the purely visual relationships in nature, but the photographs become a powerful, evocative tool only when complemented by an intellectual grasp of ecological relationships. As a photographer I seek a purity of uncluttered vision, but the goal is to instill an enlightened message, a sense of place that is whole, connected, and of value.

Symbolically I have come home again, to a past life and familiar place, but now with an important difference — a chance to share it through these images. Fortunately, I do not have to decide between the voices of the mountain waterfalls or those of the coastal tide, for both are in impressive evidence in South Carolina. It is a place worthy of continued protection and celebration. This book may be finished, but the photography is never complete.

— Tom Blagden, Jr.